BLESSING

JERUSALEM

ALL YEAR ROUND

Petra van der Zande

Photo's: Davka Corp 1998 & Petra van der Zande

ISBN 978 965 91615 7 7

Tags:
Israel; intercession, Jewish Feasts, Jerusalem, Bible study, blessing.

Email: tsurtsinapublications@gmail.com

Website: (Essence of Rock)
http://christinaboerma.com/christinaboerma

INTRODUCTION

In 1996, our Dutch friend Corrie Oosterhuis was in Calcutta, India, to intercede for the country. She had a good time, but noticed that many believers spoke negatively about the big city. Wouldn't it be wonderful if people began proclaiming living words, from God's Word, over the city instead?, Corrie thought.

Thus the 'Blessing Calendar for the City' was born, with a blessing for each day of the year. In the years that followed, this special calendar was used for big cities in general. Each time Corrie visited a major city, she left a copy of this blessing calendar behind.

When our friend visited Israel in 2010, we too received a copy of the "Blessing Calendar for the City". My suggestion to make a book with blessings specifically for Jerusalem came as an answer to prayer and confirmation to Corrie.

The Dutch publication was soon followed by an English version, and now this unique 'calendar' is also available in German, Spanish, Portuguese. More translations are being prepared.

We hope and pray that you will enjoy using this practical tool to bless the City of the Great King - Jerusalem.

I will bless those who bless you,
And I will curse him who curses you;
And in you all the families
of the earth shall be blessed.
Genesis 12:3

How does this calendar work?

Every **first** day of the month we pray for the peace of Jerusalem. The **second** day, believers and churches of the city are blessed. On the **tenth** day of the month we pray for the peace and prosperity of Jerusalem. The **eleventh** day, we bring the leaders and government before God's throne.

On the **twentieth** day, we pray for the widows, orphans and strangers living in the city. The **thirtieth** and **thirty-first** day of each month are always the same: we bless the city whose God is the LORD and look forward to the time that Jerusalem will receive a new name which means: City of God

Most of the days mentioned above use the same Scripture verses. January starts with Bible verses from the book of Genesis, and December ends with the book Revelation.

The original "Blessing Calendar" only gave Scripture references. This book contains the Bible verses, taken from the New King James Version, but it is always good to keep your Bible at hand, and read the verses in their context. Sometimes another Bible version gives a fresh insight to the blessing you proclaim over the City of the Great King.

The LORD bless you out of Zion,
And may you see
the good of Jerusalem
All the days of your life.

Psalm 128:5

Pray for the peace of Jerusalem:

"May they prosper who love you.
Peace be within your walls,
Prosperity within your palaces."
For the sake of my brethren and companions, I will
now say,
"Peace be within you."
Because of the house
of the LORD our God
I will seek your good.
Psalm 122:6-9

JERUSALEM AND THE FEASTS OF THE LORD

In Leviticus 23: 1-44 we read how the Lord God gave the Jewish people her Feasts.

In Biblical times, the Jewish New Year (Rosh Hashanah) began with the commemoration of the Exodus from Egypt. Centuries later, Rosh Hashanah was celebrated around the month of September.

Religious Jews follow the Jewish calendar, which is based on moon-months, while the Western world uses the Gregorian calendar. This is the reason why the start of the Jewish holidays is different each year. In Israel, a new day starts at sunset, when three stars can be seen in the sky.

In general terms, we can say that Pesach (Passover) usually falls in April; Shavuot (Feast of Weeks, Pentecost) usually in May; September/October is the month in which Rosh Hashanah is celebrated, and Yom Kippur (Day of Atonement) and Sukkot (Feast of Tabernacles).

Pesach, Shavuot and Sukkot were the so-called Pilgrims-feast. Three times a year, all Jewish males had to appear before God in Zion, to celebrate the "Feast of the Lord".

Purim (from 'pur', which means lot) is not a "Feast of the Lord," but is celebrated with much joy, usually in March. The Scroll of Esther is being read in the synagogue.

Memorial days are of utmost importance to the Jewish people.
On Yom haShoah they commemorate the six million Jews who were murdered by the Nazis during the Second World War. Yom haZikaron is the day we remember the soldiers who gave their lives fighting Israel's many wars, but also the victims of terror. These memorial days usually are in May.

Jerusalem was and always will be the central place for many Jewish people around the world to celebrate their holidays and Feasts.

In this calendar, the month in which a Jewish Feast is celebrated, contains additional information.

By the blessing
of the upright
the city is exalted.
Proverbs 11:11

JANUARY

Blessed be the LORD out of Zion,
Who dwells in Jerusalem!
Praise the LORD!
Psalm 135:21

JANUARY

1. PRAY FOR THE PEACE OF JERUSALEM.
Pray for the peace of Jerusalem: "May they prosper who love you.
Psalm 122:6

2. MAY GOD POUR OUT HIS SPIRIT ON THE BELIEVERS
And I will not hide My face from them anymore; for I shall have poured out
My Spirit on the house of Israel,' says the Lord GOD. Ezekiel 39:29

3. May Jerusalem be a city of light.
Then God said, "Let there be light"; and there was light. Genesis 1:3

4. May God give you of heaven's dew and of the earth's richness.
Therefore may God give you of the dew of heaven, of the fatness of the
earth, and plenty of grain and wine. Genesis 27:28

5. May the LORD be your strength and song.
The LORD is my strength and song. Exodus 15:2

6. May God become your salvation.
And He has become my salvation; He is my God, and I will praise Him; My
father's God, and I will exalt Him. Exodus 15:2

7. God will be an enemy to your enemies.
But if you indeed obey His voice and do all that I speak, then I will be an
enemy to your enemies and an adversary to your adversaries.
Exodus 23:22

8. God knows you by name and you have found favour with Him.
Then Moses said to the LORD, "See, You say to me, 'Bring up this people.'
But You have not let me know whom You will send with me. Yet You have
said, 'I know you by name, and you have also found grace in My sight.'
Exodus 33:12

9. The LORD's presence will go with you, and He will give you rest.
And He said, "My Presence will go with you, and I will give you rest."
Exodus 33:14

10. SEEK THE PEACE AND PROSPERITY OF JERUSALEM.
And seek the peace of the city where I have caused you to be carried away
captive, and pray to the LORD for it; for in its peace you will have peace.
Jeremiah 29:7

11. MAY YOUR RULERS NOT RULE OVER YOU RUTHLESSLY, BUT IN THE
FEAR OF GOD.
You shall not rule over him with rigor, but you shall fear your God.
Leviticus 25:43

12. God can break the bars of your yoke.
I am the LORD your God, who brought you out of the land of Egypt, that
you should not be their slaves; I have broken the bands of your yoke...
Leviticus 26:13

13. God can enable you to walk with heads held high.
I am the LORD your God, who brought you out of the land of Egypt, that
you should not be their slaves; …. and made you walk upright
Leviticus 26:13

14. The LORD's arm is not too short.
And the LORD said to Moses, "Has the LORD's arm been shortened? Now
you shall see whether what I say will happen to you or not."
Numbers 11:23

15. The LORD bless you, Jerusalem!
The LORD bless you and keep you; Numbers 6:24

16. The LORD wants to be gracious to you, o Jerusalem!
The LORD make His face shine upon you, and be gracious to you;
Numbers 6:25

Your watchmen shall lift up their voices,
With their voices they shall sing together;
For they shall see eye to eye
When the LORD brings back Zion.
Isaiah 52: 8

17. The LORD wants to give you peace, Jerusalem!
The LORD lift up His countenance upon you, And give you peace.
Numbers 6:26

18. May God be your praise.
He is your praise, and He is your God, who has done for you these great
and awesome things which your eyes have seen. Deuteronomy 10:21

19. May the LORD give you victory over your enemies.
For the LORD your God is He who goes with you, to fight for you against
your enemies, to save you. Deuteronomy 20:4

20. MAY THE RIGHTOUS PROSPER, SO THAT JERUSALEM REJOICES.
When it goes well with the righteous, the city rejoices; and when the
wicked perish, there is jubilation. Proverbs 11:10

21. PRAY FOR THE CAUSE OF THE FATHERLESS AND THE WIDOW, AND
THE ALIEN.
He administers justice for the fatherless and the widow, and loves the
stranger, giving him food and clothing. Deuteronomy 10:18

22. May the LORD be your life.
That you may love the LORD your God, that you may obey His voice, and
that you may cling to Him, for He is your life and the length of your days;
and that you may dwell in the land which the LORD swore to your fathers,
to Abraham, Isaac, and Jacob, to give them. Deuteronomy 30:20

23. The LORD won't leave you, o Jerusalem!
Be strong and of good courage, do not fear nor be afraid of them; for the
LORD your God, He is the One who goes with you. He will not leave you
nor forsake you. Deuteronomy 31:6

24. May God shield you and care for you.
He found him in a desert land and in the wasteland, a howling wilderness;
He encircled him, He instructed him. Deuteronomy 32:10

25. May God guard you as the apple of His eye.
He kept him as the apple of His eye. Deuteronomy 32:10

26. Let Jerusalem live and not die.
Let Reuben live, and not die, nor let his men be few. Deuteronomy 33:6

27. O LORD, be the city's help against her foes!
And this he said of Judah: "Hear, LORD, the voice of Judah, And bring him to his people; Let his hands be sufficient for him, and may You be a help against his enemies." Deuteronomy 33:7

28. Bless the work of her hands.
Bless his substance, LORD, and accept the work of his hands; Strike the loins of those who rise against him, And of those who hate him, that they rise not again. Deuteronomy 33:11

29. May Jerusalem be secure.
Of Benjamin he said: "The beloved of the LORD shall dwell in safety by Him, Who shelters him all the day long; And he shall dwell between His shoulders." Deuteronomy 33:12

30. BLESSED IS THE CITY WHOSE GOD IS THE LORD.
Blessed is the nation whose God is the LORD, The people He has chosen as His own inheritance. Psalm 33:12

31. May the name of the city be: THE LORD IS THERE
And the name of the city from that day shall be: THE LORD IS THERE." Ezekiel 48:35

NOTES

FEBRUARY

© Davka 1998

"Sing and rejoice,
O daughter of Zion!
For behold, I am coming
and I will dwell in your midst,"
says the LORD.
Zecharia 2:10

FEBRUARY

1. PRAY FOR THE PEACE OF JERUSALEM.
Pray for the peace of Jerusalem: "May they prosper who love you.
Psalm 122:6

2. MAY GOD STRENGTHEN THE BELIEVERS.
I will strengthen the house of Judah, and I will save the house of Joseph.
I will bring them back, because I have mercy on them. They shall be as
though I had not cast them aside; For I am the LORD their God, and I will
hear them. Zechariah 10:6

3. May God bless the city.
With the precious fruits of the sun, with the precious produce of the
months. Deuteronomy 33:14

4. May the earth's best gifts be brought to you.
With the precious things of the earth and its fullness, and the favor of
Him who dwelt in the bush. Let the blessing come 'on the head of Joseph,
and on the crown of the head of him who was separate from his brothers.
Deuteronomy 33:16

5. May the LORD favour Jerusalem.
And of Naphtali he said: "O Naphtali, satisfied with favor, and full of the
blessing of the LORD, possess the west and the south."
Deuteronomy 33:23

6. May God be your eternal refuge.
The eternal God is your refuge, and underneath are the everlasting arms;
He will thrust out the enemy from before you, and will say, 'Destroy!'
Deuteronomy 33:27

7. May you be blessed, Jerusalem!
Happy are you, O Israel! Who is like you, a people saved by the LORD, the
shield of your help and the sword of your majesty! Your enemies shall
submit to you, and you shall tread down their high places.
Deuteronomy 33:29

8. May God fight for you.
One man of you shall chase a thousand, for the LORD your God is He who fights for you, as He promised you. Joshua 23:10

9. Sing praises to the LORD!
Hear, O kings! Give ear, O princes! I, even I, will sing to the LORD; I will sing praise to the LORD God of Israel. Judges 5:3

10. SEEK THE PEACE AND PROSPERITY OF JERUSALEM.
And seek the peace of the city where I have caused you to be carried away captive, and pray to the LORD for it; for in its peace you will have peace. Jeremiah 29:7

11. MAY YOUR LEADERS RULE IN THE FEAR OF GOD.
The God of Israel said, The Rock of Israel spoke to me: 'He who rules over men must be just, ruling in the fear of God. 2 Samuel 23:3

12. Recite God's righteous acts.
Far from the noise of the archers, among the watering places, there they shall recount the righteous acts of the LORD, the righteous acts for His villagers in Israel; Then the people of the LORD shall go down to the gates. Judges 5:11

13. May your enemies perish, o Jerusalem!
Thus let all Your enemies perish, O LORD! Judges 5:31

14. Bless those who love the LORD.
But let those who love Him be like the sun when it comes out in full strength. Judges 5:31

15. The LORD be with you and bless you.
Now behold, Boaz came from Bethlehem, and said to the reapers, "The LORD be with you!" And they answered him, "The LORD bless you!" Ruth 2:4

Pray for
Jerusalem's
Arab population

16. May the LORD renew your life and sustain you.
And may he be to you a restorer of life and a nourisher of your old age; for your daughter-in-law, who loves you, who is better to you than seven sons, has borne him. Ruth 4:15

17. He will guard the feet of His saints.
He will guard the feet of His saints, but the wicked shall be silent in darkness. For by strength no man shall prevail. 1 Samuel 2:9

18. May the LORD be your rock, fortress and deliverer.
The LORD is my rock and my fortress and my deliverer; 2 Samuel 22:2

19. May God be your saviour.
The God of my strength, in whom I will trust; My shield and the horn of my salvation, My stronghold and my refuge; My Savior, You save me from violence. 2 Samuel 22:3

20. MAY THE RIGHTEOUS PROSPER, SO THAT JERUSALEM REJOICES.
When it goes well with the righteous, the city rejoices; and when the wicked perish, there is jubilation. Proverbs 11:10

21. MAY THE LORD RAISE THE POOR AND LIFT THE NEEDY.
He raises the poor from the dust and lifts the beggar from the ash heap, to set them among princes and make them inherit the throne of glory. "For the pillars of the earth are the LORD's, and He has set the world upon them. 1 Samuel 2:8

22. Show Yourself merciful to Jerusalem, LORD.
With the merciful You will show Yourself merciful; With a blameless man You will show Yourself blameless; 2 Samuel 22:26

23. May God turn your darkness into light.
For You are my lamp, O LORD; The LORD shall enlighten my darkness 2 Samuel 22:29

24. May the LORD arm you with strength.
God is my strength and power, And He makes my way perfect.
2 Samuel 22:33

25. May God train your hands for battle.
He teaches my hands to make war, so that my arms can bend a bow of bronze. 2 Samuel 22:35

26. May the LORD rescue you.
He delivered me from my strong enemy, from those who hated me; For they were too strong for me. 2 Samuel 22:18

27. May Jerusalem be a safe place to live.
And Judah and Israel dwelt safely, each man under his vine and his fig tree, from Dan as far as Beersheba, all the days of Solomon. 1 Kings 4:25

28. May the eyes of the LORD always be on you.
And the LORD said to him: "I have heard your prayer and your supplication that you have made before Me; I have consecrated this house which you have built to put My name there forever, and My eyes and My heart will be there perpetually. 1 Kings 9:3

29. BLESSED IS THE CITY WHOSE GOD IS THE LORD.
Blessed is the nation whose God is the LORD, The people He has chosen as His own inheritance. Psalm 33:12

רח׳ שַׁמַּאי
شارع شماي
SHAMAI ST.

NOTES

22

MARCH

Golden Gate with Muslim graves

*Then the moon will be disgraced
and the sun ashamed;
For the LORD of hosts will reign
on Mount Zion and in Jerusalem
and before His elders, gloriously.
Isaiah 24:23*

Jewish holidays in March

Purim —Esther 9: 22-24

These were the days in which the Jews were saved from their enemies. Mourning and sorrow turned into joy. The Jews were told to celebrate and send gifts to the poor. Throughout the ages, they adhered to Morchechai's advice and celebrated. In doing so, they kept memory alive of the time that the Jew-hater Haman, wanted to destroy the Jewish people.

MARCH

1. PRAY FOR THE PEACE OF JERUSALEM.
Pray for the peace of Jerusalem: "May they prosper who love you.
Psalm 122:6

2. MAY GOD POUR OUT A SPIRIT OF GRACE AND SUPPLICATION ON THE BELIEVERS.
And I will pour on the house of David and on the inhabitants of Jerusalem the Spirit of grace and supplication; then they will look on Me whom they pierced. Yes, they will mourn for Him as one mourns for his only son, and grieve for Him as one grieves for a firstborn. Zechariah 12:10

3. Deliver Jerusalem from her enemies, O LORD!
Now therefore, O LORD our God, I pray, save us from his hand, that all the kingdoms of the earth may know that You are the LORD God, You alone.
2 Kings 19:19

4. May God defend the city.
For I will defend this city, to save it for My own sake and for My servant David's sake. 2 Kings 19:34

5. May the people be blessed in the Name of the LORD.
And when David had finished offering the burnt offerings and the peace offerings, he blessed the people in the name of the LORD.
1 Chronicles 16:2

6. May those who seek You, rejoice.
Glory in His holy name; Let the hearts of those rejoice who seek the LORD.
1 Chronicles 16:10

7. May Jerusalem look to God.
Seek the LORD and His strength; Seek His face evermore.
1 Chronicles 16:11

8. May you be praised and feared, O LORD.
For the LORD is great and greatly to be praised; He is also to be feared above all gods. 1 Chronicles 16:25

9. May God be your father.
I will be his Father, and he shall be My son; and I will not take My mercy away from him, as I took it from him who was before you.
1 Chronicles 17:13

10. SEEK THE PEACE AND PROSPERITY OF JERUSALEM.
And seek the peace of the city where I have caused you to be carried away captive, and pray to the LORD for it; for in its peace you will have peace.
Jeremiah 29:7

11. MAY MANY WORK FOR THE GOOD OF JERUSALEM AND SPEAK UP FOR THE WELFARE OF THE CITIZENS
For Mordecai the Jew was second to King Ahasuerus, and was great among the Jews and well received by the multitude of his brethren, seeking the good of his people and speaking peace to all his countrymen. Esther 10:3

12. May God never take away His love for you.
I will be his Father, and he shall be My son; and I will not take My mercy away from him, as I took it from him who was before you.
1 Chronicles 17:13

13. May those who seek You, find You.
As for you, my son Solomon, know the God of your father, and serve Him with a loyal heart and with a willing mind; for the LORD searches all hearts and understands all the intent of the thoughts. If you seek Him, He will be found by you; but if you forsake Him, He will cast you off forever.
1 Chronicles 28:9

14. Bless the priests (Cohanim) and believers of Jerusalem.
Now therefore, arise, O LORD God, to Your resting place, You and the ark of Your strength. Let Your priests, O LORD God, be clothed with salvation, and let Your saints rejoice in goodness. 2 Chronicles 6:41

15. Bless those who are fully committed to you.
For the eyes of the LORD run to and fro throughout the whole earth, to show Himself strong on behalf of those whose heart is loyal to Him. In this you have done foolishly; therefore from now on you shall have wars.
2 Chronicles 16:9

16. May Jerusalem seek You, O LORD.
So Judah gathered together to ask help from the LORD; and from all the cities of Judah they came to seek the LORD. 2 Chronicles 20:4

17. May God's hand be upon you.
And has extended mercy to me before the king and his counselors, and before all the king's mighty princes. So I was encouraged, as the hand of the LORD my God was upon me; and I gathered leading men of Israel to go up with me. Ezra 7:28

18. May God give you light and relief.
And now for a little while grace has been shown from the LORD our God, to leave us a remnant to escape, and to give us a peg in His holy place, that our God may enlighten our eyes and give us a measure of revival in our bondage. Ezra 9:8

19. May God be merciful.
And I commanded the Levites that they should cleanse themselves, and that they should go and guard the gates, to sanctify the Sabbath day. Remember me, O my God, concerning this also, and spare me according to the greatness of Your mercy! Nehemiah 13:22

20. MAY THE RIGHTOUS PROSPER, SO THAT JERUSALEM REJOICES. When it goes well with the righteous, the city rejoices; and when the wicked perish, there is jubilation. Proverbs 11:10

21. MAY THE RIGHTEOUS CARE ABOUT JUSTICE FOR THE POOR. The righteous considers the cause of the poor, but the wicked does not understand such knowledge. Proverbs 29:7

22. May you be pure and upright.
If you were pure and upright, surely now He would awake for you, and prosper your rightful dwelling place. Job 8:6

23. May your future be prosperous.
Though your beginning was small, yet your latter end would increase abundantly. Job 8:7

24. May your mouth be filled with laughter.
He will yet fill your mouth with laughing, and your lips with rejoicing. Job 8:21

25. May you have many intercessors as your friends.
My friends scorn me; My eyes pour out tears to God. Job 16:20

26. May the breath of the Almighty give you life.
The Spirit of God has made me, and the breath of the Almighty gives me life. Job 33:4

27. May you delight in the law of the LORD.
But his delight is in the law of the LORD, and in His law he meditates day and night. Psalm 1:2

28. May God Most High be your defence.
My defense is of God, Who saves the upright in heart. Psalm 7:10

29. May the LORD save and defend you.
May the LORD answer you in the day of trouble; May the name of the God of Jacob defend you. Psalm 20:1

30. BLESSED IS THE CITY WHOSE GOD IS THE LORD.
Blessed is the nation whose God is the LORD, The people He has chosen as His own inheritance. Psalm 33:12

31. May the name of the city be: THE LORD IS THERE

And the name of the city from that day shall be: "THE LORD IS THERE."
Ezekiel 48:35

 NOTES

APRIL

Archaeological Park and Mt. of Olives with Jewish graves.

For the people shall dwell in Zion at Jerusalem;
You shall weep no more.
He will be very gracious to you
at the sound of your cry;
When He hears it, He will answer you.
Isaiah 30:19

Jewish holidays in April

Leviticus 23:4-6

These are the feasts of the LORD, holy convocations which you shall proclaim at their appointed times. On the fourteenth day of the first month at twilight is the LORD's Passover. And on the fifteenth day of the same month is the Feast of Unleavened Bread to the LORD; seven days you must eat unleavened bread.

APRIL

1. PRAY FOR THE PEACE OF JERUSALEM
Pray for the peace of Jerusalem: "May they prosper who love you.
Psalm 122:6

2. MAY THE BELIEVERS BE UNITED.
I in them, and You in Me; that they may be made perfect in one, and that the world may know that You have sent Me, and have loved them as You have loved Me. John 17:23

3. May God fulfil your heart's desire.
May He grant you according to your heart's desire, And fulfil all your purpose. Psalm 20:4

4. May the LORD be your shepherd.
The LORD is my shepherd; I shall not want. He restores my soul; He leads me in the paths of righteousness or His name's sake. Psalm 23:1,3

5. May you have clean hands and a pure heart.
He who has clean hands and a pure heart, who has not lifted up his soul to an idol, nor sworn deceitfully. He shall receive blessing from the LORD, and righteousness from the God of his salvation. Psalm 24:4,5

6. O LORD, be gracious to the city.
Turn Yourself to me, and have mercy on me, for I am desolate and afflicted. Psalm 25:16

7. May you not be afraid, O Jerusalem!
The LORD is my light and my salvation; Whom shall I fear? The LORD is the strength of my life; Of whom shall I be afraid? Psalm 27:1

8. May the LORD lead you in a straight path.
Teach me Your way, O LORD, and lead me in a smooth path, because of my enemies. Psalm 27:11

9. Bless your people, Lord, and give them strength.
The LORD will give strength to His people; The LORD will bless His people with peace. Psalm 29:11

10. SEEK THE PEACE AND PROSPERITY OF JERUSALEM
And seek the peace of the city where I have caused you to be carried away captive, and pray to the LORD for it; for in its peace you will have peace. Jeremiah 29:7

11. MAY THE RULERS DISTINGUISH BETWEEN RIGHT AND WRONG.
Therefore give to Your servant an understanding heart to judge Your people, that I may discern between good and evil. For who is able to judge this great people of Yours? 1 Kings 3:9

12. May God be your deliverer.
You are my hiding place; You shall preserve me from trouble; You shall surround me with songs of deliverance. Selah. Psalm 32:7

13. Bless the meek, LORD.
But the meek shall inherit the earth, and shall delight themselves in the abundance of peace. Psalm 37:11

14. May Jerusalem trust in the LORD.
Blessed is that man who makes the LORD his trust, and does not respect the proud, nor such as turn aside to lies. Psalm 40:4

15. A river that makes the city of God glad.
There is a river whose streams shall make glad the city of God, the holy place of the tabernacle of the Most High. Psalm 46:4

16. May the LORD bless you, Jerusalem!
The LORD bless you, Jerusalem! God be merciful to us and bless us, and cause His face to shine upon us, Selah. Psalm 67:1

17. Bless them whose strength is in You.
Blessed is the man whose strength is in You, whose heart is set on pilgrimage. Psalm 84:5

18. Show the city your unfailing love, LORD.
Show us Your mercy, LORD, and grant us Your salvation. Psalm 85:7

19. Bless those who seek You.
Blessed are those who keep His testimonies, who seek Him with the whole heart! Psalm 119:2

20. MAY THE RIGHTOUS PROSPER, SO THAT JERUSALEM REJOICES.
When it goes well with the righteous, the city rejoices; and when the wicked perish, there is jubilation. Proverbs 11:10

21. BLESS THOSE WHO REGARD THE WEAK.
Blessed is he who considers the poor; The LORD will deliver him in time of trouble. Psalm 41:1

22. May the LORD do great things.
The LORD has done great things for us, and we are glad. Psalm 126:3

23. May the watchmen not guard in vain!
Unless the LORD builds the house, they labour in vain who build it; Unless the LORD guards the city, the watchman stays awake in vain.
Psalm 127:1

24 . May Jerusalemites live in unity.
Behold, how good and how pleasant it is for brethren to dwell together in unity! Psalm 133:1

25. May Jerusalem know that our LORD is greater than all gods.
For I know that the LORD is great, and our Lord is above all gods.
Psalm 135:5

26. May the LORD fulfil His purpose for you.
The LORD will perfect that which concerns me; Your mercy, O LORD, endures forever; Do not forsake the works of Your hands Psalm 138:8

27. May God have compassion on you.
The LORD is good to all, and His tender mercies are over all His works. Psalm 145:9

28. Praise the LORD, Jerusalem!
Let the high praises of God be in their mouth, and a two-edged sword in their hand, Psalm 149:6

29. Let everything that has breath praise the LORD.
Let everything that has breath praise the LORD. Praise the LORD! Psalm 150:6

30. BLESSED IS THE CITY WHOSE GOD IS THE LORD.
Blessed is the nation whose God is the LORD, The people He has chosen as His own inheritance. Psalm 33:12

NOTES

MAY

But Judah shall abide forever,
And Jerusalem from generation to generation.
For I will acquit them of the guilt of bloodshed,
whom I had not acquitted;
For the LORD dwells in Zion.

Joël 3:20,21

Jewish holidays in May

Leviticus 23:9-11; 15,16

And the LORD spoke to Moses...'When you come into the land which I give to you, and reap its harvest, then you shall bring a sheaf of the firstfruits of your harvest to the priest.... on the day after the Sabbath the priest shall wave it....And you shall count for yourselves from the day after the Sabbath, from the day that you brought the sheaf of the wave offering: seven Sabbaths shall be completed. Count fifty days to the day after the seventh Sabbath; then you shall offer a new grain offering to the LORD.

MAY

1. PRAY FOR THE PEACE OF JERUSALEM
Pray for the peace of Jerusalem: "May they prosper who love you.
Psalm 122:6

2. MAY THE BELIEVERS ENJOY THE FAVOUR OF ALL PEOPLE
Praising God and having favor with all the people. And the Lord added to
the church daily those who were being saved. Acts 2:47

3. May you have discretion and understanding.
Discretion will preserve you; Understanding will keep you. Proverbs 2:11

4. Have mercy and follow the truth.
Let not mercy and truth forsake you; Bind them around your neck, write
them on the tablet of your heart. Proverbs 3:3

5. May the LORD keep you.
For the LORD will be your confidence, and will keep your foot from being
caught. Proverbs 3:26

6. Fear the LORD.
The fear of the LORD is the beginning of wisdom, and the knowledge of
the Holy One is understanding. Proverbs 9:10

7. LORD, remember the righteous.
The LORD will not allow the righteous soul to famish, but He casts away
the desire of the wicked. Proverbs 10:3

8. May the LORD bless the righteous.
Blessings are on the head of the righteous, but violence covers the mouth
of the wicked. Proverbs 10:6

9. May the LORD be a refuge for the righteous.
The way of the LORD is strength for the upright, but destruction will
come to the workers of iniquity. Proverbs 10:29

10. SEEK THE PEACE AND PROSPERITY OF JERUSALEM
And seek the peace of the city where I have caused you to be carried away captive, and pray to the LORD for it; for in its peace you will have peace. Jeremiah 29:7

11. MAY GOD ENDOW THE RULERS WITH JUSTICE AND RIGHTEOUSNESS.
Give the king Your judgments, O God, and Your righteousness to the king's Son. Psalm 72:1

12. May all fear You, O God.
The fear of the LORD is a fountain of life, to turn one away from the snares of death. Proverbs 14:27

13. Bless those who pursue righteousness.
The way of the wicked is an abomination to the LORD, but He loves him who follows righteousness. Proverbs 15:9

14. Bless those who trust in You, O LORD.
He who heeds the word wisely will find good, and whoever trusts in the LORD, happy is he. Proverbs 16:20

15. May the righteous run to the LORD.
The name of the LORD is a strong tower; the righteous run to it and are safe. Proverbs 18:10

16. May Jerusalem fear the LORD.
The fear of the LORD leads to life, and he who has it will abide in satisfaction; He will not be visited with evil. Proverbs 19:23

17. May justice be done in Jerusalem.
It is a joy for the just to do justice, but destruction will come to the workers of iniquity. Proverbs 21:15

18. May Jerusalem know humility and the fear of the LORD.
By humility and the fear of the LORD are riches and honor and life. Proverbs 22:4

19. May the guilty be convicted.
But those who rebuke the wicked will have delight, and a good blessing will come upon them. Proverbs 24:25

20. MAY THE RIGHTOUS PROSPER, SO THAT JERUSALEM REJOICES.
When it goes well with the righteous, the city rejoices; and when the wicked perish, there is jubilation. Proverbs 11:10

21. SPEAK UP FOR THE RIGHTS OF THE DESTITUTE.
Open your mouth for the speechless, in the cause of all who are appointed to die Proverbs 31:8

22. May Jerusalem trust in the LORD.
He who is of a proud heart stirs up strife, but he who trusts in the LORD will be prospered. Proverbs 28:25

23. May God be your shield.
Every word of God is pure; He is a shield to those who put their trust in Him. Proverbs 30:5

24. May the wise save the city by their wisdom.
Now there was found in it a poor wise man, and he by his wisdom delivered the city. Yet no one remembered that same poor man. Ecclesiastes 9:15

25. May Jerusalem know wisdom.
Wisdom is good with an inheritance. And profitable to those who see the sun. Ecclesiastes 7:11

26. May the youth of the city remember their Creator.
Remember now your Creator in the days of your youth, before the difficult days come, and the years draw near when you say, " I have no pleasure in them". Ecclesiastes 12:1

27. May Jerusalem be a fragrant city.
Because of the fragrance of your good ointments, Your name is ointment poured forth; Therefore the virgins love you. Song of Solomon 1:3

Zechor!

Zechor!

REMEMBER!

REMEMBER!

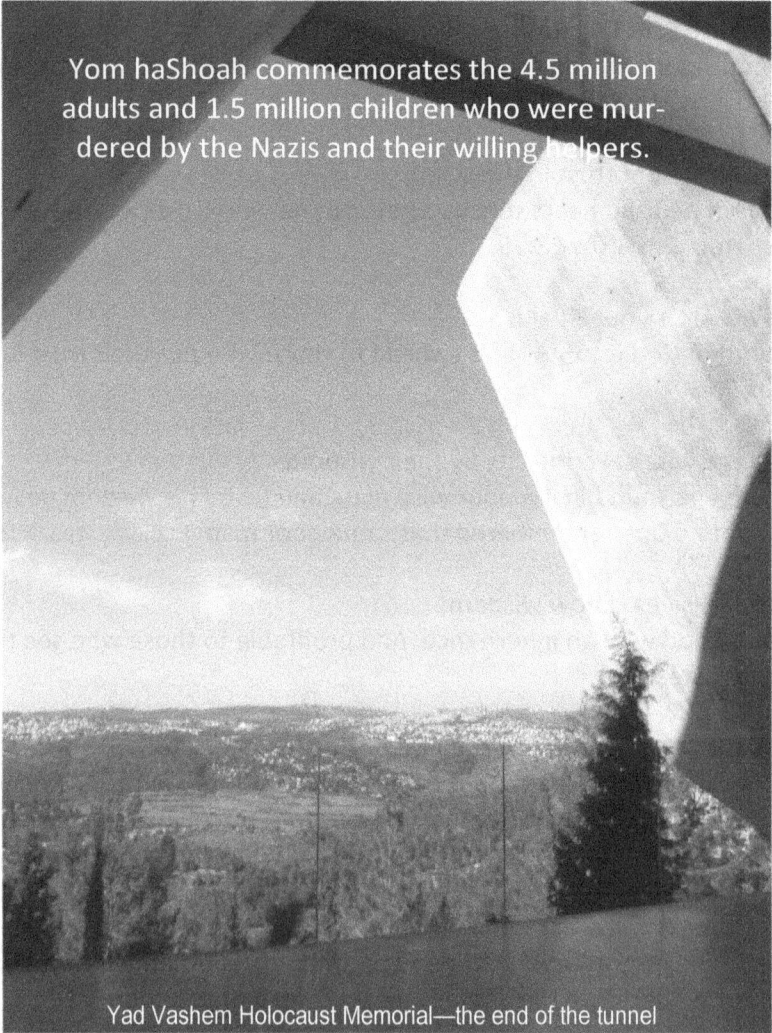

Yom haShoah commemorates the 4.5 million adults and 1.5 million children who were murdered by the Nazis and their willing helpers.

Yad Vashem Holocaust Memorial—the end of the tunnel

To forget means to die, to remember, to live

Thousands of fallen soldiers on the IDF cemetery on Mt. Herzl.

28. May Jerusalem be like an apple tree among the trees.
Like an apple tree among the trees of the woods, so is my beloved among the sons. I sat down in his shade with great delight, and his fruit was sweet to my taste. Song of Solomon 2:3

29. How beautiful you are, O city of God!
Behold, you are fair, my love! Behold, you are fair! You have dove's eyes behind your veil. Your hair is like a flock of goats, going down from Mount Gilead. Song of Solomon 4:1

30. BLESSED IS THE CITY WHOSE GOD IS THE LORD.
Blessed is the nation whose God is the LORD, The people He has chosen as His own inheritance. Psalm 33:12

31. May the name of the city be: THE LORD IS THERE
And the name of the city from that day shall be: THE LORD IS THERE."
Ezekiel 48:35

Jemin Moshe

NOTES

JUNE

View from Mount Scopus direction Old City

For the LORD has chosen Zion;
He has desired it for His dwelling place.
Psalm 132:13

JUNE

1. PRAY FOR THE PEACE OF JERUSALEM
Pray for the peace of Jerusalem: "May they prosper who love you.
Psalm 122:6

2. MAY THE BELIEVERS STAND FIRM IN THEIR FAITH.
The head of Ephraim is Samaria, and the head of Samaria is Remaliah's son.
If you will not believe, surely you shall not be established. Isaiah 7:9

3. May you be called: City of righteousness and Faithful city.
I will restore your judges as at the first, and your counselors as at the
beginning. Afterward you shall be called the city of righteousness, the
faithful city. Isaiah 1:26

4. May the righteous enjoy the fruit of their deeds.
Say to the righteous that it shall be well with them, for they shall eat the
fruit of their doings. Isaiah 3:10

5. May those who walk in darkness see the Light.
The people who walked in darkness have seen a great light; Those who
dwelt in the land of the shadow of death, upon them a light has shined.
Isaiah 9:2

6. May the LORD free you from the oppressor.
You have multiplied the nation and increased its joy; They rejoice before
You according to the joy of harvest, as men rejoice when they divide the
spoil. Isaiah 9:4

7. May the LORD be your salvation.
Behold, God is my salvation, I will trust and not be afraid; ' For YAH, the
LORD, is my strength and song; He also has become my salvation.
Isaiah 12:2

8. May you draw water from the wells of salvation.
Therefore with joy you will draw water from the wells of salvation.
Isaiah 12:3

9. May all turn their eyes to the Holy One of Israel.
In that day a man will look to his Maker, and his eyes will have respect for the Holy One of Israel. Isaiah 17:7

10. SEEK THE PEACE AND PROSPERITY OF JERUSALEM.
And seek the peace of the city where I have caused you to be carried away captive, and pray to the LORD for it; for in its peace you will have peace.
Jeremiah 29:7

11. MAY JERUSALEM'S RULERS GIVE STABILITY BY JUSTICE.
The king establishes the land by justice, but he who receives bribes overthrows it. Proverbs 29:4

12. May God be a source of strength.
For a spirit of justice to him who sits in judgment, and for strength to those who turn back the battle at the gate. Isaiah 28:6

13. May you act just and righteously.
Also I will make justice the measuring line, and righteousness the plummet.
Isaiah 28:17

14. Repent, rest and trust, O Jerusalem!
For thus says the Lord GOD, the Holy One of Israel: "In returning and rest you shall be saved; In quietness and confidence shall be your strength."
Isaiah 30:15

15. May the LORD be gracious and show mercy.
Therefore the LORD will wait, that He may be gracious to you; And therefore He will be exalted, that He may have mercy on you. Isaiah 30:18

16. May Jerusalem wait for the LORD.
For the LORD is a God of justice; Blessed are all those who wait for Him.
Isaiah 30:18

17. May the LORD be your salvation.
O LORD, be gracious to us; We have waited for You. Be their arm every morning, our salvation also in the time of trouble Isaiah 33:2

18. May the LORD be your sure foundation.
Wisdom and knowledge will be the stability of your times, and the strength of salvation. Isaiah 33:6

19. May the city be blessed with the fear of the LORD.
The fear of the LORD is His treasure. Isaiah 33:6

20. MAY THE RIGHTOUS PROSPER, SO THAT JERUSALEM REJOICES.
When it goes well with the righteous, the city rejoices; and when the wicked perish, there is jubilation. Proverbs 11:10

21. SPEAK UP AND JUDGE FAIRLY; DEFEND THE RIGHTS OF THE POOR AND NEEDY.
Open your mouth, judge righteously, and plead the cause of the poor and needy. Proverbs 31:9

22. That many may walk on the Way of Holiness.
A highway shall be there, and a road, and it shall be called the Highway of Holiness. The unclean shall not pass over it, but it shall be for others. Whoever walks the road, although a fool, shall not go astray. Isaiah 35:8

23. Do not fear, O Jerusalem!
Fear not, for I am with you; Be not dismayed, for I am your God. I will strengthen you, yes, I will help you, I will uphold you with My righteous right hand.' Isaiah 41:10

24. May the LORD nourish the people.
For I will pour water on him who is thirsty, and floods on the dry ground; I will pour My Spirit on your descendants, and My blessing on your offspring; Isaiah 44:3

25. May God go before you and level the mountains.
I will go before you and make the crooked places straight. Isaiah 45:2

26. May God break down gates of bronze.
I will break in pieces the gates of bronze and cut the bars of iron.
Isaiah 45:2

27. May the LORD comfort the city.
Break forth into joy, sing together, you waste places of Jerusalem! For the
LORD has comforted His people, He has redeemed Jerusalem.
Isaiah 52:9

28. May you bless the lowly in spirit.
For thus says the High and Lofty One Who inhabits eternity, whose name is
Holy: " I dwell in the high and holy place, with him who has a contrite and
humble spirit, to revive the spirit of the humble, and to revive the heart of
the contrite ones. Isaiah 57:15

29. May God extend peace like a river.
For thus says the LORD: " Behold, I will extend peace to her like a river, and
the glory of the Gentiles like a flowing stream. Then you shall feed; On her
sides shall you be carried, and be dandled on her knees. Isaiah 66:12

30. BLESSED IS THE CITY WHOSE GOD IS THE LORD.
Blessed is the nation whose God is the LORD, The people He has chosen as
His own inheritance. Psalm 33:12

Looking towards the Valley of Jehoshaphat.

NOTES

JULY

Old City, Armenian Quarter

What will they answer the messengers of the nation?
That the LORD has founded Zion,
And the poor of His people shall take refuge in it.
Isaiah 14:32

JULY

1. PRAY FOR THE PEACE OF JERUSALEM
Pray for the peace of Jerusalem: "May they prosper who love you.
Psalm 122:6

2. MAY THE BELIEVERS BE ONE IN HEART AND MIND.
Now the multitude of those who believed were of one heart and one soul;
neither did anyone say that any of the things he possessed was his own, but
they had all things in common. Acts 4:32

3. May you walk in the ways of the LORD.
But this is what I commanded them, saying, 'Obey My voice, and I will be
your God, and you shall be My people. And walk in all the ways that I have
commanded you, that it may be well with you.' Jeremiah 7:23

4. May there be a time of healing.
We looked for peace, but no good came; and for a time of health, and there
was trouble! Jeremiah 8:15

5. May the LORD deliver you for a good purpose.
The LORD said: " Surely it will be well with your remnant; Surely I will cause
the enemy to intercede with you in the time of adversity and in the time of
affliction. Jeremiah 15:11

6. May God's words be your joy and delight.
Your words were found, and I ate them, and Your word was to me the joy
and rejoicing of my heart; For I am called by Your name, O LORD God of
hosts. Jeremiah 15:16

7. May the LORD rescue and save you.
And I will make you to this people a fortified bronze wall; And they will fight
against you, but they shall not prevail against you; For I am with you to save
you and deliver you, says the LORD. Jeremiah 15:20

8. May Jerusalem trust in the LORD.
Blessed is the man who trusts in the LORD, and whose hope is the LORD.
Jeremiah 17:7

9. May the LORD be with you.
But the LORD is with me as a mighty, awesome One. Therefore my
persecutors will stumble, and will not prevail. They will be greatly ashamed,
for they will not prosper. Their everlasting confusion will never be forgotten.
Jeremiah 20:11

10. SEEK THE PEACE AND PROSPERITY OF JERUSALEM.
And seek the peace of the city where I have caused you to be carried away
captive, and pray to the LORD for it; for in its peace you will have peace.
Jeremiah 29:7

11. MAY GOD MAKE PEACE YOUR GOVERNOR AND RIGHTEOUSNESS YOUR
RULER.
Instead of bronze I will bring gold, instead of iron I will bring silver, instead
of wood, bronze, and instead of stones, iron. I will also make your officers
peace, and your magistrates righteousness. Isaiah 60:17

12. Nothing is too hard for You, O LORD.
"Behold, I am the LORD, the God of all flesh. Is there anything too hard for
Me? Jeremiah 32:27

13. May the LORD be your God, O Jerusalem.
They shall be My people, and I will be their God; Jeremiah 32:38

14. May your future be full of hope.
For I know the thoughts that I think toward you, says the LORD, thoughts of
peace and not of evil, to give you a future and a hope. Jeremiah 29:11

15. May the LORD be your portion.
" The LORD is my portion," says my soul, " Therefore I hope in Him!"
Lamentations 3:24

16. May you seek the LORD.
The LORD is good to those who wait for Him, to the soul who seeks Him.
Lamentations 3:25

17. May God set the ensnared free.
'Therefore thus says the Lord GOD: "Behold, I am against your magic charms
by which you hunt souls there like birds. I will tear them from your arms, and
let the souls go, the souls you hunt like birds. Ezekiel 13:20

18. May God make your beauty complete.
Your fame went out among the nations because of your beauty, for it was
perfect through My splendor which I had bestowed on you," says the Lord
GOD. Ezekiel 16:14

19. May you know the LORD.
And I will establish My covenant with you. Then you shall know that I am the
LORD, Ezekiel 16:62

20. MAY THE RIGHTOUS PROSPER.
When it goes well with the righteous, the city rejoices; and when the wicked
perish, there is jubilation. Proverbs 11:10

21. DELIVER THE NEEDY AND THE AFFLICTED.
For He will deliver the needy when he cries, the poor also, and him who has
no helper Psalm 72:12

22. May there be showers of blessing upon the city.
I will make them and the places all around My hill a blessing; and I will cause
showers to come down in their season; there shall be showers of blessing.
Ezekiel 34:26

23. May God rescue you from your enslavers.
Then the trees of the field shall yield their fruit, and the earth shall yield her
increase. They shall be safe in their land; and they shall know that I am the
LORD, when I have broken the bands of their yoke and delivered them from
the hand of those who enslaved them. Ezekiel 34:27

24. May God look at you with favour.
For indeed I am for you, and I will turn to you, and you shall be tilled and sown. Ezekiel 36:9

25. May you no longer suffer disgrace among the nations.
And I will multiply the fruit of your trees and the increase of your fields, so that you need never again bear the reproach of famine among the nations. Ezekiel 36:30

26. May God's dwelling place be with you.
My tabernacle also shall be with them; indeed I will be their God, and they shall be My people. Ezekiel 37:27

27. May Your holy Name be known.
So I will make My holy name known in the midst of My people Israel, and I will not let them profane My holy name anymore. Then the nations shall know that I am the LORD, the Holy One in Israel. Ezekiel 39:7

28. May the LORD have compassion on the city.
"Therefore thus says the Lord GOD: 'Now I will bring back the captives of Jacob, and have mercy on the whole house of Israel; and I will be jealous for My holy name— Ezekiel 39:25

29 . May God look after His sheep.
'For thus says the Lord GOD: "Indeed I Myself will search for My sheep and seek them out. Ezekiel 34:11

30. BLESSED IS THE CITY WHOSE GOD IS THE LORD.
Blessed is the nation whose God is the LORD, The people He has chosen as His own inheritance. Psalm 33:12

31. May the name of the city be: THE LORD IS THERE
And the name of the city from that day shall be: THE LORD IS THERE." Ezekiel 48:35

Jerusalem's
many
faces

NOTES

AUGUST

New Gate to the Christian Quarter

Awake, awake! Put on your strength, O Zion;
Put on your beautiful garments,
O Jerusalem, the holy city!
For the uncircumcised and the unclean
Shall no longer come to you.
Isaiah 52:1

AUGUST

1. PRAY FOR THE PEACE OF JERUSALEM
Pray for the peace of Jerusalem: "May they prosper who love you.
Psalm 122:6

2. MAY THE BELIEVERS ENJOY A TIME OF PEACE
Then the churches throughout all Judea, Galilee, and Samaria had peace
and were edified. And walking in the fear of the Lord and in the comfort of
the Holy Spirit, they were multiplied. Acts 9:31

3. May you prosper greatly.
Nebuchadnezzar the king, To all peoples, nations, and languages that dwell
in all the earth: Peace be multiplied to you. Daniel 4:1

4. May God rescue and save you.
He delivers and rescues, and He works signs and wonders in heaven and on
earth, who has delivered Daniel from the power of the lions.
Daniel 6:27

5. O LORD, look favourably to Jerusalem.
Now therefore, our God, hear the prayer of Your servant, and his supplications, and for the Lord's sake cause Your face to shine on Your sanctuary,
which is desolate. Daniel 9:17

6. May your wise shine.
Those who are wise shall shine like the brightness of the firmament,
Daniel 12:3

7. May those who are righteous shine.
And those who turn many to righteousness like the stars forever and
ever. Daniel 12:3

8. May God show love and favour to the city.
Yet I will have mercy on the house of Judah, will save them by the LORD
their God, and will not save them by bow, nor by sword or battle, by horses
or horsemen. Hosea 1:7

9. May God make the Valley of Achor a door of hope.
I will give her her vineyards from there, and the Valley of Achor as a door of hope; She shall sing there, as in the days of her youth, as in the day when she came up from the land of Egypt. Hosea 2:15

10. SEEK THE PEACE AND PROSPERITY OF JERUSALEM.
And seek the peace of the city where I have caused you to be carried away captive, and pray to the LORD for it; for in its peace you will have peace. Jeremiah 29:7

11. PRAY FOR THE WELL-BEING OF THE MAYOR AND HIS FAMILY
That they may offer sacrifices of sweet aroma to the God of heaven, and pray for the life of the king and his sons. Ezra 6:10

12. May the LORD come like spring rains.
Let us know, let us pursue the knowledge of the LORD. His going forth is established as the morning; He will come to us like the rain, like the latter and former rain to the earth. Hosea 6:3

13. May the LORD lead you with cords of human kindness.
I drew them with gentle cords, with bands of love. Hosea 11:4

14. May the LORD care for you.
And I was to them as those who take the yoke from their neck. I stooped and fed them. Hosea 11:4

15. May you experience righteousness, justice, loving-kindness and mercy.
I will betroth you to Me forever; Yes, I will betroth you to Me in righteousness and justice, in loving-kindness and mercy. Hosea 2:19

16. May God pour out His spirit on the people.
" And it shall come to pass afterward that I will pour out My Spirit on all flesh; Your sons and your daughters shall prophesy, your old men shall dream dreams, your young men shall see visions. Joel 2:28

17. May the LORD be a refuge and stronghold.
The LORD also will roar from Zion, and utter His voice from Jerusalem;
The heavens and earth will shake; But the LORD will be a shelter for His
people, and the strength of the children of Israel. Joel 3:16

18. May God water the city.
And it will come to pass in that day that the mountains shall drip with new
wine, the hills shall flow with milk, and all the brooks of Judah shall be
flooded with water; A fountain shall flow from the house of the LORD And
water the Valley of Acacias. Joel 3:18

19. May the LORD dwell in the city.
For I will acquit them of the guilt of bloodshed, whom I had not acquitted;
For the LORD dwells in Zion." Joel 3:21

20. MAY THE RIGHTOUS PROSPER, SO THAT JERUSALEM REJOICES.
When it goes well with the righteous, the city rejoices; and when the
wicked perish, there is jubilation. Proverbs 11:10

21. FOR IN GOD THE FATHERLESS FIND COMPASSION.
Assyria shall not save us, we will not ride on horses, nor will we say
anymore to the work of our hands, 'You are our gods.' For in You the
fatherless finds mercy." Hosea 14:3

22. May justice roll like a river.
But let justice run down like water, and righteousness like a mighty
stream. Amos 5:24

23. May God restore the city.
On that day I will raise up the tabernacle of David, which has fallen down,
and repair its damages; I will raise up its ruins, and rebuild it as in the days
of old; Amos 9:11

24. Let there be deliverance and holiness in the city.
But on Mount Zion there shall be deliverance, and there shall be holiness;
The house of Jacob shall possess their possessions. Obadiah 17

25. May God bring your life up from the pit.
I went down to the moorings of the mountains; The earth with its bars
closed behind me forever; Yet You have brought up my life from the pit,
O LORD, my God. Jonah 2:6

26. Salvation comes from the LORD.
But I will sacrifice to You with the voice of thanksgiving; I will pay what I
have vowed. Salvation is of the LORD. Jonah 2:9

27. May your ways be upright.
You who are named the house of Jacob: Is the Spirit of the LORD restricted?
Are these His doings? Do not My words do good to him who walks
uprightly? Micah 2:7

28. May your people walk in the Name of our LORD.
For all people walk each in the name of his god, but we will walk in the name
of the LORD our God forever and ever. Micah 4:5

29. May God be your peace.
And He shall stand and feed His flock in the strength of the LORD,
In the majesty of the name of the LORD His God; And they shall abide,
For now He shall be great to the ends of the earth; And this One shall be
peace. Micah 5:4,5

30. BLESSED IS THE CITY WHOSE GOD IS THE LORD.
Blessed is the nation whose God is the LORD, The people He has chosen as
His own inheritance. Psalm 33:12

31. May the name of the city be: THE LORD IS THERE
And the name of the city from that day shall be: THE LORD IS THERE."
Ezekiel 48:35

Do good in Your good pleasure to Zion;
Build the walls of Jerusalem.
Psalm 51:18

NOTES

SEPTEMBER

High Court of Justice, Jerusalem
© Davka 1998

Many nations shall come and say,
"Come, and let us go up
to the mountain of the LORD,
To the house of the God of Jacob;
He will teach us His ways,
And we shall walk in His paths."
For out of Zion the law shall go forth,
And the word of the LORD from Jerusalem.
Micha 4:2

Jewish Feasts in September

Leviticus 23:23-27

Then the LORD spoke to Moses, saying, 'In the seventh month, on the first day of the month, you shall have a sabbath-rest, a memorial of blowing of trumpets, a holy convocation. You shall do no customary work on it; and you shall offer an offering made by fire to the LORD.'" "Also the tenth day of this seventh month shall be the Day of Atonement. It shall be a holy convocation for you; you shall afflict your souls...

SEPTEMBER

1. PRAY FOR THE PEACE OF JERUSALEM.
Pray for the peace of Jerusalem: "May they prosper who love you.
Psalm 122:6

2. MAY BELIEVERS SPREAD THE FRAGRANCE OF CHRIST.
Now thanks be to God who always leads us in triumph in Christ, and
through us diffuses the fragrance of His knowledge in every place.
2 Corinthians 2:14

3. May the LORD care for you, Jerusalem.
The LORD is good, a stronghold in the day of trouble; And He knows those
who trust in Him. Nahum 1:7

4. May many come to the city to proclaim peace.
Behold, on the mountains the feet of him who brings good tidings, who
proclaims peace! O Judah, keep your appointed feasts, perform your
vows. For the wicked one shall no more pass through you; He is utterly
cut off. Nahum 1:15

5. May the LORD restore the splendour of the city.
For the LORD will restore the excellence of Jacob like the excellence of
Israel, For the emptiers have emptied them out and ruined their vine
branches. Nahum 2:2

6. May the righteous live by faith.
Behold the proud, his soul is not upright in him; But the just shall live by
his faith. Habakkuk 2:4

7. May Jerusalem be filled with the knowledge of the LORD.
For the earth will be filled with the knowledge of the glory of the LORD,
as the waters cover the sea. Habakkuk 2:14

8. May the LORD be your strength.
The LORD God is my strength; He will make my feet like deer's feet, and He will make me walk on my high hills. Habakkuk 3:19

9. Seek the LORD, O Jerusalem!
Seek the LORD, all you meek of the earth, who have upheld His justice. Seek righteousness, seek humility. It may be that you will be hidden in the day of the LORD's anger. Zephaniah 2:3

10. SEEK THE PEACE AND PROSPERITY OF JERUSALEM.
And seek the peace of the city where I have caused you to be carried away captive, and pray to the LORD for it; for in its peace you will have peace. Jeremiah 29:7

11. MAY THE RULERS MAKE JUST LAWS.
By me kings reign, and rulers decree justice. Proverbs 8:15

12. May the LORD care for you.
The coast shall be for the remnant of the house of Judah; They shall feed their flocks there; For the LORD their God will intervene for them, and return their captives. Zephaniah 2:7

13. Purify the lips of the people, LORD.
For then I will restore to the peoples a pure language, that they all may call on the name of the LORD, to serve Him with one accord. Zephaniah 3:9

14. May the LORD take away your punishment.
Sing, O daughter of Zion! Shout, O Israel! Be glad and rejoice with all your heart, O daughter of Jerusalem! The LORD has taken away your judgments, He has cast out your enemy. The King of Israel, the LORD, is in your midst; You shall see disaster no more. Zephaniah 3:14,15

15. May the LORD be with you.
The LORD your God in your midst, the Mighty One, will save; He will rejoice over you with gladness. Zephaniah 3:17

16. May the LORD rejoice in you.
He will quiet you with His love, He will rejoice over you with singing."
Zephaniah 3:17

17. May the glory of this present city be greater than the former.
'The glory of this latter temple shall be greater than the former,' says the
LORD of hosts. Haggai 2:9

18. May the LORD grant peace to Jerusalem.
'And in this place I will give peace,' says the LORD of hosts." Haggai 2:9

19. May God be a wall of fire around the city.
For I,' says the LORD, 'will be a wall of fire all around her, and I will be the
glory in her midst.'" Zechariah 2:5

20. MAY THE RIGHTOUS PROSPER, SO THAT JERUSALEM REJOICES.
When it goes well with the righteous, the city rejoices; and when the wicked
perish, there is jubilation. Proverbs 11:10

21. BLESS THE WIDOW, FATHERLESS, ALIEN AND POOR.
Do not oppress the widow or the fatherless, the alien or the poor. Let none
of you plan evil in his heart against his brother.' Zechariah 7:10

22. May Jerusalem experience Your power, O LORD.
So he answered and said to me: " This is the word of the LORD to
Zerubbabel: ' Not by might nor by power, but by My Spirit,' says the LORD
of hosts. Zechariah 4:6

23. May Jerusalem be called the 'city of Truth'.
"Thus says the LORD: ' I will return to Zion, and dwell in the midst of
Jerusalem. Jerusalem shall be called the City of Truth, the Mountain of the
LORD of hosts, the Holy Mountain.' Zechariah 8:3

24. May God be faithful and righteous to you.
I will bring them back, and they shall dwell in the midst of Jerusalem. They
shall be My people and I will be their God, in truth and righteousness.'
Zechariah 8:8

25. May there be sound judgement in your courts.
These are the things you shall do: speak each man the truth to his neighbour; Give judgment in your gates for truth, justice, and peace; Zechariah 8:16

26. You are the Apple of God's eye!
For thus says the LORD of hosts: "He sent Me after glory, to the nations which plunder you; for he who touches you touches the apple of His eye. Zechariah 2:8

27. May there be many messengers of the LORD Almighty.
The law of truth was in his mouth, and injustice was not found on his lips. He walked with Me in peace and equity, and turned many away from iniquity. "For the lips of a priest should keep knowledge, and people should seek the law from his mouth; For he is the messenger of the LORD of hosts. Malachi 2:6,7

28. May your blessings overflow.
Bring all the tithes into the storehouse, that there may be food in My house, and try Me now in this," says the LORD of hosts, " If I will not open for you the windows of heaven and pour out for you such blessing that there will not be room enough to receive it. Malachi 3:10

29. May you experience healing, O Jerusalem!
But to you who fear My name the Sun of Righteousness shall arise with healing in His wings; And you shall go out and grow fat like stall-fed calves. Malachi 4:2

30. BLESSED IS THE CITY WHOSE GOD IS THE LORD.
Blessed is the nation whose God is the LORD, The people He has chosen as His own inheritance. Psalm 33:12

So the angel who spoke with me said to me, "Proclaim, saying, 'Thus says the LORD of hosts: 'I am zealous for Jerusalem And for Zion with great zeal. Zecharia 1:14

NOTES

OCTOBER

Central synagogue   © Davka 199[8]

" Rejoice greatly, O daughter of Zion!
Shout, O daughter of Jerusalem!
Behold, your King is coming to you;
He is just and having salvation, Lowly and riding on a donkey,
A colt, the foal of a donkey.
Zechariah 9:9

" Tell the daughter of Zion,' Behold, your King is coming to you,
Lowly, and sitting on a donkey, A colt, the foal of a donkey.'"
Matthew 21:5

Jewish Holidays in October

Leviticus 23:33,34

Then the LORD spoke to Moses, saying, 'The fifteenth day of this seventh month shall be the Feast of Tabernacles for seven days to the LORD. On the first day there shall be a holy convocation. You shall do no customary work on it. On the eighth day you shall have a holy convocation...

OCTOBER

1. PRAY FOR THE PEACE OF JERUSALEM.
Pray for the peace of Jerusalem: "May they prosper who love you.
Psalm 122:6

2. MAY GOD BLESS THE BELIEVERS WITH EVERY SPIRITUAL BLESSING IN CHRIST.
Blessed be the God and Father of our Lord Jesus Christ, who has blessed us with every spiritual blessing in the heavenly places in Christ. Ephesians 1:3

3. Bless the poor in spirit.
Blessed are the poor in spirit, for theirs is the kingdom of heaven.
Matthew 5:3

4. Bless those who mourn.
Blessed are those who mourn, for they shall be comforted. Matthew 5:4

5. Bless the meek.
Blessed are the meek, for they shall inherit the earth. Matthew 5:5

6. Bless those who seek righteousness.
Blessed are those who hunger and thirst for righteousness, for they shall be filled. Matthew 5:6

7. Bless the merciful.
Blessed are the merciful, for they shall obtain mercy. Matthew 5:7

8. Bless the pure in heart.
Blessed are the pure in heart, for they shall see God. Matthew 5:8

9. Bless the peacemakers. Blessed are the peacemakers, for they shall be called sons of God. Matthew 5:9

10. SEEK THE PEACE AND PROSPERITY OF JERUSALEM.
And seek the peace of the city where I have caused you to be carried away captive, and pray to the LORD for it; for in its peace you will have peace. Jeremiah 29:7

11. KEEP THOSE WHO ARE FAITHFUL.
Mercy and truth preserve the king, and by loving-kindness he upholds his throne. Proverbs 20:28

12. May the Jerusalem's children be blessed.
And He took them up in His arms, laid His hands on them, and blessed them. Mark 10:16

13. May those who are rich find God.
Then Jesus looked around and said to His disciples, "How hard it is for those who have riches to enter the kingdom of God!" Mark 10:23

14. Bless the blind people of the city.
And when he heard that it was Jesus of Nazareth, he began to cry out and say, "Jesus, Son of David, have mercy on me!" Mark 10:47

15. May those who suffer find peace.
And He said to her, "Daughter, your faith has made you well. Go in peace, and be healed of your affliction." Mark 5:34

16. Bless those who believe in God's Word.
Blessed is she who believed, for there will be a fulfilment of those things which were told her from the Lord." Luke 1:45

17. May God's mercy be on those who fear Him.
And His mercy is on those who fear Him from generation to generation. Luke 1:50

18. May God rescue you from your enemies.
To grant us that we, being delivered from the hand of our enemies, might serve Him without fear, in holiness and righteousness before Him all the days of our life. Luke 1:74,75

19. May Yeshua be a light to the Gentiles.
A light to bring revelation to the Gentiles, and the glory of Your people Israel. Luke 2:32

20. MAY THE RIGHTOUS PROSPER, SO THAT JERUSALEM REJOICES.
When it goes well with the righteous, the city rejoices; and when the wicked perish, there is jubilation. Proverbs 11:10

21. MAY THE LORD FILL THE HUNGRY
He has filled the hungry with good things, and the rich He has sent away empty. Luke 1:53

22. May there be many who have great faith.
When Jesus heard these things, He marvelled at him, and turned around and said to the crowd that followed Him, "I say to you, I have not found such great faith, not even in Israel." Luke 7:9

23. Bless the Messianic believers.
And blessed is he who is not offended because of Me. Luke 7:23

24. May you be filled with God's grace.
And of His fullness we have all received, and grace for grace. John 1:16

25. May Yeshua be the Bread of Life for Jerusalem.
And Jesus said to them, "I am the bread of life. He who comes to Me shall never hunger, and he who believes in Me shall never thirst. John 6:35

26. May Yeshua be the Light of Jerusalem.
As long as I am in the world, I am the light of the world." John 9:5

27. Bless Yeshua, the Good Shepherd.
"I am the good shepherd. The good shepherd gives His life for the sheep. John 10:11

PRAYER FOR RAIN

'And it shall be that if you earnestly obey My commandments which I command you today, to love the LORD your God and serve Him with all your heart and with all your soul, then I will give you the rain for your land in its season, the early rain and the latter rain, that you may gather in your grain, your new wine, and your oil.
Deuteronomy 11: 13,14

On the last day of the Feast of Tabernacles, religious Jews begin to pray for rain.

The *Joreh,* the first rain after the long, dry summer, usually begins to fall near the end of October, beginning of November and is always a reason for joy and gratefulness. The fields can be ploughed and pre-pared for next year's harvests.

Geshem are the winter rains, sometimes pouring down between mid-December till March.

Melkosh is the Hebrew name for the 'latter rains', falling in spring and needed to help grow the barley and grain.

Showers over Gilo,
seen from Ramat Denia

28. Bless those who found that Yeshua is the Way.
Jesus said to him, "I am the way, the truth, and the life. No one comes to the Father except through Me. John 14:6

29. May the Spirit of Truth guide many.
However, when He, the Spirit of truth, has come, He will guide you into all truth; for He will not speak on His own authority, but whatever He hears He will speak; and He will tell you things to come. John 16:13

30. BLESSED IS THE CITY WHOSE GOD IS THE LORD.
Blessed is the nation whose God is the LORD, The people He has chosen as His own inheritance. Psalm 33:12

31. May the name of the city be: THE LORD IS THERE
And the name of the city from that day shall be: THE LORD IS THERE." Ezekiel 48:35

NOTES

83

NOVEMBER

Mount of Olives with Church of Ascension

Also the sons of those who afflicted you
Shall come bowing to you,
And all those who despised you
shall fall prostrate at the soles of your feet;
And they shall call you The City of the LORD,
Zion of the Holy One of Israel.
Isaiah 60:14

NOVEMBER

1. PRAY FOR THE PEACE OF JERUSALEM.
Pray for the peace of Jerusalem: "May they prosper who love you.
Psalm 122:6

2. MAY GOD FILL THE BELIEVERS WITH KNOWLEDGE OF HIS WILL.
For this reason we also, since the day we heard it, do not cease to pray for you, and to ask that you may be filled with the knowledge of His will in all wisdom and spiritual understanding; Colossians 1:9

3. Blessed are those who have not seen and yet believed.
Jesus said to him, "Thomas, because you have seen Me, you have believed. Blessed are those who have not seen and yet have believed." John 20:29

4. May many join together in prayer.
These all continued with one accord in prayer and supplication, with the women and Mary the mother of Jesus, and with His brothers. Acts 1:14

5. May many repent and be baptised.
Then Peter said to them, "Repent, and let every one of you be baptized in the name of Jesus Christ for the remission of sins; and you shall receive the gift of the Holy Spirit. Acts 2:38

6. May the LORD enable the believers to speak His Word with boldness.
Now, Lord, look on their threats, and grant to Your servants that with all boldness they may speak Your word. Acts 4:29

7. May there be many miraculous signs in the city.
And through the hands of the apostles many signs and wonders were done among the people. And they were all with one accord in Solomon's Porch…. And believers were increasingly added to the Lord, multitudes of both men and women, Acts 5:12,14

8. May the number of believers increase.
Then the word of God spread, and the number of the disciples multiplied greatly in Jerusalem, and a great many of the priests were obedient to the faith. Acts 6:7

9. May many see that their sins can be forgiven through Yeshua.
Therefore let it be known to you, brethren, that through this Man is preached to you the forgiveness of sins; Acts 13:38

10. SEEK THE PEACE AND PROSPERITY OF JERUSALEM.
And seek the peace of the city where I have caused you to be carried away captive, and pray to the LORD for it; for in its peace you will have peace. Jeremiah 29:7

11. MAY THE GOVERNMENT JUDGE THE POOR WITH FAIRNESS
The king who judges the poor with truth, His throne will be established forever. Proverbs 29:14

12. May the Word of the LORD spread through the city.
And the word of the Lord was being spread throughout all the region. Acts 13:49

13. May the LORD fill your hearts with joy.
Nevertheless He did not leave Himself without witness, in that He did good, gave us rain from heaven and fruitful seasons, filling our hearts with food and gladness." Acts 14:17

14. May many find peace in Yeshua.
Therefore, having been justified by faith, we have peace with God through our Lord Jesus Christ, Romans 5:1

15. May many receive God's Spirit. But you are not in the flesh but in the Spirit, if indeed the Spirit of God dwells in you. Now if anyone does not have the Spirit of Christ, he is not His. Romans 8:9

16. May You work for the good of those who love You, LORD.
And we know that all things work together for good to those who love God, to those who are the called according to His purpose. Romans 8:28

17. If God is for you, who can be against you, O Jerusalem?
What then shall we say to these things? If God is for us, who can be against us? Romans 8:31

18. May nothing separate you from the love of God.
nor height nor depth, nor any other created thing, shall be able to separate us from the love of God which is in Christ Jesus our Lord. Romans 8:39

19. May the LORD bless those who call on Him.
For there is no distinction between Jew and Greek, for the same Lord over all is rich to all who call upon Him. For "whoever calls on the name of the LORD shall be saved." Romans 10:12,13

20. MAY THE RIGHTOUS PROSPER, SO THAT JERUSALEM REJOICES.
When it goes well with the righteous, the city rejoices; and when the wicked perish, there is jubilation. Proverbs 11:10

21. TO KNOW GOD IS TO DEFEND THE CAUSE OF THE POOR AND NEEDY.
He judged the cause of the poor and needy; Then it was well. Was not this knowing Me? says the LORD. Jeremiah 22:16

22. May God give you endurance and encouragement.
Now may the God of patience and comfort grant you to be like-minded toward one another, according to Christ Jesus, Romans 15:5

23. May you glorify God with one mind and mouth.
that you may with one mind and one mouth glorify the God and Father of our Lord Jesus Christ. Romans 15:6

24. May Satan be crushed under your feet.
And the God of peace will crush Satan under your feet shortly. The grace of our Lord Jesus Christ be with you. Amen. Romans 16:20

25. May you experience hope, patience and faith.
rejoicing in hope, patient in tribulation, continuing steadfastly in prayer;
Romans 12:12

26. May many love God so that they are known by God.
But if anyone loves God, this one is known by Him. 1 Corinthians 8:3

27. May God live with you and walk with you.
And what agreement has the temple of God with idols? For you are the
temple of the living God. As God has said: " I will dwell in them And walk
among them. I will be their God, and they shall be My people."
2 Corinthians 6:16

28. May you abound in Yeshua's grace.
And God is able to make all grace abound toward you, that you, always having all sufficiency in all things, may have an abundance for every good work.
2 Corinthians 9:8

29. May you experience grace, love and fellowship.
The grace of the Lord Jesus Christ, and the love of God, and the communion
of the Holy Spirit be with you all. Amen. 2 Corinthians 13:14

30. BLESSED IS THE CITY WHOSE GOD IS THE LORD.
Blessed is the nation whose God is the LORD, The people He has chosen as
His own inheritance. Psalm 33:12

Domari (Gypsy)
children from
Jerusalem

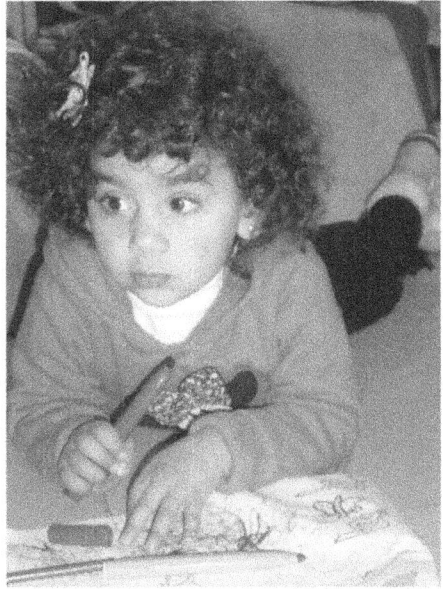

NOTES

DECEMBER

[Jerusalem] ...your life would be brighter than noonday.
Though you were dark, you would be like the morning.
And you would be secure, because there is hope;
Yes, you would dig around you,
and take your rest in safety.
You would also lie down,
and no one would make you afraid;
Yes, many would court your favour.
Job 11:17-19

Jewish holidays in December

John 10: 22-25 Jesus and Chanukah

Now it was the Feast of Dedication in Jerusalem, and it was winter. And Jesus walked in the temple, in Solomon's porch. Then the Jews surrounded Him and said to Him, "How long do You keep us in doubt? If You are the Christ, tell us plainly." Jesus answered them, "I told you, and you do not believe. The works that I do in My Father's name, they bear witness of Me.

DECEMBER

1. PRAY FOR THE PEACE OF JERUSALEM.
Pray for the peace of Jerusalem: "May they prosper who love you.
Psalm 122:6

2. MAY GOD GIVE THE BELIEVERS A SPIRIT OF POWER, LOVE AND
3. SELF-DISCIPLINE.
For God has not given us a spirit of fear, but of power and of love and of a
sound mind. 2 Timothy 1:7

3. May the fruit of the Spirit be evident in the believers.
But the fruit of the Spirit is love, joy, peace, longsuffering, kindness,
goodness, faithfulness, Galatians 5:22

4. May the manifold wisdom of God be made known.
To the intent that now the manifold wisdom of God might be made known
by the church to the principalities and powers in the heavenly places,
Ephesians 3:10

5. May Jerusalem experience God's peace.
and the peace of God, which surpasses all understanding, will guard your
hearts and minds through Christ Jesus. Philippians 4:7

6. May God's fullness be seen in Jerusalem.
For in Him dwells all the fullness of the Godhead bodily; and you are
complete in Him, who is the head of all principality and power.
Colossians 2:9,10

7. May Jerusalem be sanctified by the God of peace.
Now may the God of peace Himself sanctify you completely; and may your
whole spirit, soul, and body be preserved blameless at the coming of our
Lord Jesus Christ. 1 Thessalonians 5:23

8. May Jerusalem receive eternal encouragement and hope.
Now may our Lord Jesus Christ Himself, and our God and Father, who has
loved us and given us everlasting consolation and good hope by grace,
2 Thessalonians 2:16

9. May God's grace be poured out on Jerusalem.
And the grace of our Lord was exceedingly abundant, with faith and love
which are in Christ Jesus. 1 Timothy 1:14

10. SEEK THE PEACE AND PROSPERITY OF JERUSALEM.
And seek the peace of the city where I have caused you to be carried away
captive, and pray to the LORD for it; for in its peace you will have peace.
Jeremiah 29:7

11. BLESS JERUSALEM'S LEADERS
Therefore I exhort first of all that supplications, prayers, intercessions, and
giving of thanks be made for all men, for kings and all who are in authority,
that we may lead a quiet and peaceable life in all godliness and reverence.
1 Timothy 2:1,2

12. May God's grace bring salvation.
For the grace of God that brings salvation has appeared to all men.
Titus 2:11

13. Bless those who share their faith.
that the sharing of your faith may become effective by the
acknowledgment of every good thing which is in you in Christ Jesus.
Philemon 6

14. Bless the believers who hope without wavering.
Let us hold fast the confession of our hope without wavering, for He who
promised is faithful. Hebrews 10:23

15. May Jerusalem experience God's holiness.
For they indeed for a few days chastened us as seemed best to them, but
He for our profit, that we may be partakers of His holiness.... Pursue peace
with all people, and holiness, without which no one will see the Lord:

Hebrews 12:10,14

16. May the LORD complete the good work He began.
Now may the God of peace who brought up our Lord Jesus from the dead, that great Shepherd of the sheep, through the blood of the everlasting covenant, make you complete in every good work to do His will, working in you what is well pleasing in His sight, through Jesus Christ, to whom be glory forever and ever. Amen. Hebrews 13:20.21

17. Bless those who persevere in their trials.
Blessed is the man who endures temptation; for when he has been approved, he will receive the crown of life which the Lord has promised to those who love Him. James 1:12

18. May God make Jerusalem a steadfast city.
But may the God of all grace, who called us to His eternal glory by Christ Jesus, after you have suffered a while, perfect, establish, strengthen, and settle you. 1 Peter 5:10

19. May Jerusalem be freed from corruption.
By which have been given to us exceedingly great and precious promises, that through these you may be partakers of the divine nature, having escaped the corruption that is in the world through lust. 2 Peter 1:4

20. MAY THE RIGHTOUS PROSPER, SO THAT JERUSALEM REJOICES.
When it goes well with the righteous, the city rejoices; and when the wicked perish, there is jubilation. Proverbs 11:10

21. MAY THE PEOPLE OF JERUSALEM ENJOY GOOD HEALTH.
Beloved, I pray that you may prosper in all things and be in health, just as your soul prospers. 3 John 2

22. May the people of Jerusalem walk in God's light.
But if we walk in the light as He is in the light, we have fellowship with one another, and the blood of Jesus Christ His Son cleanses us from all sin.

1 John 1:7

23. May the people of Jerusalem walk in God's obedience.
This is love, that we walk according to His commandments. This is the commandment, that as you have heard from the beginning, you should walk in it. 2 John 6

24. May the believers be built up in faith.
But you, beloved, building yourselves up on your most holy faith, praying in the Holy Spirit, keep yourselves in the love of God, looking for the mercy of our Lord Jesus Christ unto eternal life. Jude 20,21

25. GLORY TO GOD IN THE HIGHEST
" Glory to God in the highest, and on earth peace, goodwill toward men!" Luke 2:14

26. Bless those who take God's Word to heart.
Blessed is he who reads and those who hear the words of this prophecy, and keep those things which are written in it; for the time is near. Revelation 1:3

27. Blessed are those who thirst for the Living Water.
And He said to me, "It is done! I am the Alpha and the Omega, the Beginning and the End. I will give of the fountain of the water of life freely to him who thirsts. Revelation 21:6

28. May the glory of God give Jerusalem light.
The city had no need of the sun or of the moon to shine in it, for the glory of God illuminated it. The Lamb is its light. Revelation 21:23

29. Bless those who keep God's commandments.
Blessed are those who do His commandments, that they may have the right to the tree of life, and may enter through the gates into the city. Revelation 22:14

30. BLESSED IS THE CITY WHOSE GOD IS THE LORD.
Blessed is the nation whose God is the LORD, The people He has chosen as His own inheritance. Psalm 33:12

31. May the name of the city be: THE LORD IS THERE
And the name of the city from that day shall be: THE LORD IS THERE."
Ezekiel 48:35

NOTES

CHANUKAH LESSONS

During the second century BC, Jerusalem became more and more Hellenistic. Many perceived their Jewish nationality to be of less importance than the much greater, newer Greek culture. Instead of proclaiming the unique message of Jerusalem, the city where God's Shekinah had been, the Jewish capital became a cheap imitation of Athens and Alexandria.

A small group of courageous Jews stood up against the paganism, and even though there were was only enough oil for one day, the Menorah in the Temple burnt for eight days. *Nes Gadol Haya Pôh* – a great miracle was here! That is what Chanukah is all about, and that's why we sing: *Banu choshech legarèsh* - we have come to banish the darkness!

"In every generation that are people who have turned against us and tried to annihilate us, but the Almighty, blessed be He, rescued us from their hands." (From the Pesach Hagadah.)

Throughout the ages, the Jewish people have been surrounded by darkness and experienced one tragedy after another. But even then, there always were a handful of people who said: "Let there be light!"

God's enemy still wants to destroy Jerusalem. The spiritual battle for Jerusalem has never ceased.

As non-Jewish believers, who are grafted into the olive tree (Israel), we can pray for God's power and grace to come upon the city of Jerusalem. And even more important: bless her.

And together with the Apple of God's eye, we may look forward to the New Jerusalem, which will be named:

"THE CITY WHOSE GOD IS THE LORD!"

Do not be overcome by evil,
but overcome evil with good.
Romans 12:21